WHAT'S SO
AMAZING
ABOUT GRACE?

PARTICIPANT'S GUIDE

Resources by Philip Yancey

The Jesus I Never Knew
What's So Amazing About Grace?
The Bible Jesus Read
Reaching for the Invisible God
Where Is God When It Hurts?
Disappointment with God
The Student Bible, General Edition (with Tim Stafford)
Meet the Bible (with Brenda Quinn)
Church: Why Bother?
Finding God in Unexpected Places
I Was Just Wondering
Soul Survivor
Rumors of Another World
Prayer

Books by Philip Yancey and Dr. Paul Brand

Fearfully and Wonderfully Made
In His Image
The Gift of Pain
In the Likeness of God

ZONDERVAN | groupware™

PHILIP YANCEY

WHAT'S SO AMAZING ABOUT GRACE?

PARTICIPANT'S GUIDE

written by
Brenda Quinn and Sheryl Moon

ZONDERVAN®

GRAND RAPIDS, MICHIGAN 49530 USA

ZONDERVAN.COM/
AUTHORTRACKER

ZONDERVAN®

What's So Amazing About Grace? Participant's Guide
Copyright © 2000 by Philip D. Yancey

Requests for information should be addressed to:

Zondervan, *Grand Rapids, Michigan 49530*

ISBN-10: 0-310-23325-9
ISBN-13: 978-0-310-23325-1

Printed in the United States of America

HB 05.09.2018

CONTENTS

INTRODUCTION

———⦵⦵⦵———

Little did I know what I was getting into when I began writing a book on the word *grace*. I chose the topic out of my concern that some of us in the U.S. church have lost our way and that we stand in danger of losing our most important contribution to the world. As I began my research, I came to see that grace underlies the gospel. Far from being some abstract theological doctrine, grace affects us in very practical ways: in family feuds, marital spats, even international crises.

I truly believe that the future of the church depends on how we master the art of "dispensing grace." Other groups excel at morality. Jesus taught us one great distinctive, that of grace, which has its own slow but steady power to change the world.

Thousands of churches and groups have bought and used the video series for my book *The Jesus I Never Knew*, and we have produced this video series partly in response to their encouragement. *What's So Amazing About Grace?* takes the principles I learned from Jesus and applies them in real-life, contemporary situations. Grace is not just about what happened two thousand years ago. It affects how we treat illegal aliens and former enemies, as well as outspoken pro-choice activists or other groups with whom we might disagree. It concerns what happens today, between you and your father or your unjust employer or the cranky neighbor down the street.

We have produced ten video segments (each about twelve minutes long) and a corresponding curriculum to help you take a look at grace with your class or small group. In each session, I introduce the aspect of grace we will consider, and then interviews with others expound on the theme I've introduced. Most of the material in this video series is new, so those who read the book (although it is not necessary for class participation) will find that the video enhances and further develops what they have read.

I have filled the book and this video series with stories because I believe that is the best way to comprehend grace. I hope they become springboards for your own stories. Groups are an ideal place to share stories of grace and ungrace. At its core *grace* is a relationship word.

PHILIP YANCEY

THE MISSING INGREDIENT
A BEAUTIFUL WORD,
A POWERFUL CONCEPT

Questions to Consider

- What does the word *grace* mean?

- In what ways do we see the power—and the absence—of grace in our everyday lives and in our world?

- How did Jesus model grace?

- What impact *should* grace have on our world?

A Word Packed with Meaning

What comes to mind when you hear the word *grace*?

- A religious word that draws a blank
- A word that makes me uncomfortable
- A word that gives me hope
- The story of my life
- A yearning I feel inside
- Other

What words or phrases can you think of that contain the word *grace* or some form of this word?

How would you define the word *grace*?

Video Notes

Philip Yancey: "I'm convinced that the future of the church in this new century depends on how well we master this notion of grace."

Philip Yancey: "I wrote this book because *grace* is not the first word that comes to mind when people think of Christians."

Philip Yancey: "Gordon MacDonald once said, 'Grace is the one thing the church has that you can't get anywhere else.'"

Philip Yancey: "Never, ever, underestimate the power of grace. It is a gift from God, and it holds within it a supernatural power."

Philip Yancey: "Grace is a gift, free of charge, on the house. You only have to do one thing to receive a gift: open your hands."

Bible Study

1. Read John 8:1–11, in which Jesus forgives an adulterous woman. What do you find interesting about this story?

   everyone but Jesus left the scene.

2. Read Leviticus 20:10 and Deuteronomy 22:22, in which God's law regarding adultery is given through Moses. Who else should have been punished according to God's law?

3. In the passage from John, what new attitude toward the law does God show through the person of Jesus?

   Grace

4. What effect does Jesus' grace have on the crowd? On the woman?

A Modern-Day Story

Philip Yancey heard this story from a friend who works with the down-and-out in Chicago:

A prostitute came to me in wretched straits, homeless, sick, unable to buy food for her two-year-old daughter. Through sobs and tears, she told me she had been renting out her daughter—two years old!—to men interested in kinky sex. She made more renting out her daughter for an hour than she could earn on her own in a night. She had to do it, she said, to support her own drug habit. I could hardly bear hearing her sordid story. For one thing, it made me legally liable—I'm required to report cases of child abuse. I had no idea what to say to this woman.

At last I asked if she had ever thought of going to a church for help. I will never forget the look of pure, naive shock that crossed her face. "Church!" she cried. "Why would I ever go there? I was already feeling terrible about myself. They'd just make me feel worse."

Small Group Discussion

1. Why is it so difficult to extend grace in this type of situation?

2. In what ways would our response to this modern-day prostitute parallel the Pharisees' response to the adulterous woman? How should it differ?

3. What might it look like if an individual or a church responded with grace to the prostitute's plea for help?

4. How does our church currently reach out in grace—to our members, to our community, to our world?

5. Read 2 Thessalonians 2:16–17. What impact should this verse have on our interactions with those around us?

pass on encouragement

Summary

In this session we:

- Began to think about the meaning of the word *grace*.
- Were introduced to Philip Yancey and his initial thoughts on the power of grace — and the absence of grace — in our world.
- Studied Jesus' example of grace as he interacted with the woman caught in adultery.
- Explored some of the ways we *should* be experiencing grace in our world.

Suggested Reading

For more thoughts from Philip Yancey and more stories about grace, read:

What's So Amazing About Grace? chapters 1 – 3.

These chapters include some details about Philip's personal pilgrimage toward God and grace, a retelling of the short story and movie *Babette's Feast,* an excerpt from Erma Bombeck, and an account of Philip's first experiences of grace through, surprisingly, music, nature, and romantic love.

Looking for Grace Inside Myself

1. What do I hope to gain from this study on grace?

2. When have I experienced grace, or the opposite of grace, in my life?

3. Who has modeled a grace-filled life for me? To whom do I need to extend more grace?

4. In what area of my life is God's Spirit nudging me to address an issue of grace?

Pray that God would open your heart to the areas of your life where there needs to be more grace.

19

LETTING GRACE SOAK IN
GOD'S LOVE
FOR THE UNDESERVING

—⊗⊗⊗—

Questions to Consider

- What is my perception of God as my Father?

- How did Jesus—God's Son—treat sinners?

- What can we learn from the parable of the prodigal son?

- What do we mean when we say, "God's love is unconditional"?

The Prodigal Father

What adjectives would you use to describe God as your Father?

Creator
teacher
over all
omnicient

What was your image of God like when you were growing up?

- A gentle, grandfatherly type full of love for me
- A stern, crotchety old man just waiting to punish me
- A distant deity who didn't care much about my everyday life
- I never thought about God growing up
- Other

When you were growing up, did your parents offer more of a conditional or unconditional love? How do you think your relationship with your parents has affected your perceptions of God?

Video Notes

Opening comment: "You either deserve grace, or you don't, if you ask me!"

Philip Yancey: "The more ungodly, unrighteous, undesirable a person was, the more that person felt drawn to Jesus. And the more righteous, together, and desirable a person was, the more that person felt threatened by Jesus. Just the opposite of what most people think!"

Philip Yancey: "Somehow Jesus had mastered the ability of loving people whose behavior he disapproved. That's a lesson the church has not been so good at learning."

Susan Shpytkovsky: "Yes, I've been angry, and yes it's frustrating . . . but I really feel that it's a responsibility for me . . . that I love her unconditionally. That is the promise of grace . . . that it's a gift!"

Philip Yancey: "God loves us not because of who we are but because of who God is."

Bible Study

Read Luke 15:11–32 — the parable of the prodigal son.

1. Do you relate more to the older son or the prodigal son in this parable?

2. Are there any ways in which you identify with the father?

3. Where do you think God wants you to see yourself in this story?

4. Do you think most parents today would respond to a runaway child the way the father in the parable did, running to embrace the child and throwing a welcome-home party? Do you know of anyone who has experienced a similar situation?

5. What does it take to come to a response like the father showed in the parable?

Small Group Discussion

In his book Philip writes,

The notion of God's love coming to us free of charge, no strings attached, seems to go against every instinct of humanity. The Buddhist eight-fold path, the Hindu doctrine of *karma,* the Jewish covenant, and Muslim code of law—each of these offers a way to earn approval. Only Christianity dares to make God's love unconditional.

1. What does it mean when we say, "God's love is unconditional"?

2. In what ways is the church communicating God's unconditional love? In what ways is it communicating a conditional love?

Philip also writes,

Grace means there is nothing I can do to make God love me more, and nothing I can do to make God love me less.

3. Do you agree or disagree?

In another passage Philip writes,

From nursery school onward we are taught how to succeed in the world of ungrace. Work hard for what you earn. The early bird gets the worm. No pain, no gain. There is no such thing as a free lunch. Demand your rights. Get what you pay for. I know these rules well because I live by them. I work for what I earn; I like to win; I insist on my rights. I want fairness. I want people to get what they deserve—nothing more, nothing less. Yet if I care to listen, I hear a loud whisper from the gospel that I did not get what I deserved. I deserved punishment and got forgiveness. I deserved wrath and got love.

4. What is your reaction?

5. Why is "fairness" such a key issue for us?

6. God extends his grace to us as a gift. What does it take to receive it?

Summary

In this session we:

- Identified our perceptions of God as our Father.
- Were reminded by Philip Yancey of Jesus' unconditional acceptance of sinners.
- Evaluated grace in our lives in light of the lessons we learn from the parable of the prodigal son.
- Discovered that God's unconditional love comes to us as a free gift—with no strings attached. All we need to do is open our hands to receive it.

Suggested Reading

For more thoughts from Philip Yancey and more stories about grace, read:

What's So Amazing About Grace? chapters 4–5.

These chapters include a story about C. S. Lewis, four modern-day parables, an account of a magazine column Philip Yancey wrote which was considered by some readers to be blasphemous, and a lesson learned in the final seconds of an NCAA basketball championship.

Looking for Grace Inside Myself

1. When has God shown great love to me during a time of sin or waywardness?

2. Who are the "prodigals" in my life — in my family, in my circle of friends, in our church fellowship? How can I reach out to them with the grace of Jesus?

3. When has someone whom I have hurt or offended shown grace to me?

4. Is God's Spirit prompting me to respond in love toward someone who has wronged me?

Pray that you will be open to the individuals in your life with whom you need to heal a relationship. Ask God to give you an opportunity to begin the healing process.

AN UNNATURAL ACT
EXTENDING GRACE WHEN YOU'VE BEEN WRONGED

———⸛———

Questions to Consider

- Why is forgiving so difficult?

- Why is forgiveness important?

- How is grace related to forgiveness?

The Most Difficult Act

What are some of the wrongs we see committed that are difficult for us to forgive?

If a person is a committed Christian who genuinely loves God, why is forgiveness still so difficult at times?

Video Notes

Philip Yancey: "I know of nothing harder than forgiveness, and also nothing more urgent. Jesus was blunt. 'Your Father will forgive you,' he said, 'as you forgive others.'"

Lewis Smedes: When you forgive:

1. You surrender your right to get even.

2. You give your enemy's humanity back.

3. You get the freedom to wish that person well.

4. You are willing to be open to what God wills.

Philip Yancey: "Forgiveness has supernatural power. It works in the forgiving party. It works in the forgiven party. And in an extraordinary act of linkage, it brings the two together."

Pardoxy of not forgiving:
"you live w/ the hurt each time
you revisit the incident"

you get the freedom

Bible Study

1. Read Psalm 103:8–12 and Psalm 145:8–9. What do these verses tell us about God's grace toward us?

2. Read Romans 1:5 and Romans 6:14. What do these verses tell us about God's grace and our salvation?

3. Read 1 Corinthians 1:4 and Ephesians 2:8–9. What do these verses tell us about the source of our grace?

4. Read Ephesians 4:31–32. What do these verses teach us about our grace toward others?

5. Based on all of these Scriptures, where does forgiveness come from?

Discussion Questions

In his book Philip writes,

All too often I drift back into a tit-for-tat struggle that slams the door on forgiveness. *Why should I make the first move? I was the one wronged.* So I make no move, and cracks in the relationship appear, then widen. In time a chasm yawns open that seems impossible to cross. I feel sad, but seldom do I accept the blame. Instead, I justify myself and point out the small gestures I made toward reconciliation. I keep a mental accounting of those attempts so as to defend myself if I am ever blamed for the rift. I flee from the risk of grace to the security of ungrace.

1. Do you think this is a typical situation? Why or why not?

2. Why does this way of handling a relationship not bring reconciliation?

3. Why is grace a "risk"?

4. When is it the most difficult for you to forgive someone? When is it easiest?

When is it the most difficult for you to ask forgiveness? When is it easiest?

5. Why is it that only through God's power can we forgive and heal the relationships in our lives?

Summary

In this session we:

- Considered the great difficulty involved in forgiving.
- Examined why it is so important for us to forgive.
- Ascertained that many times forgiveness is impossible without grace.

Suggested Reading

For more thoughts from Philip Yancey and more stories about grace, read:

What's So Amazing About Grace? chapters 6–7.

These chapters include a story about unforgiveness that spanned three generations in one family; an account of a weekend Philip Yancey spent with ten Jews, ten Christians, and ten Muslims, led by M. Scott Peck; and an excerpt from Henri Nouwen.

Looking for Grace Inside Myself

1. Do I practice forgiveness fairly regularly and consistently, or is forgiveness toward one who has wronged me usually difficult?

2. Choosing to forgive often means taking the initiative. Do I more often take the initiative or more often wait for the other person to make the first move?

3. Is God's Spirit nudging me to take the initiative in healing a relationship with someone I need to forgive?

Pray for courage to take the first step in mending that relationship. Ask God to give you graceful words and open ears.

THE ART OF FORGIVING
RESPONDING WITH GRACE
WHEN IT SEEMS IMPOSSIBLE

———⊶∞⊷———

Questions to Consider

- How does an unforgiving spirit enslave us?

- Is forgiveness ever inappropriate or impossible?

The Act That Sets Us Free

When someone does something to offend us or hurt our feelings (or our egos!), why is it our natural tendency to hold on to the offense and let it turn into a grudge?

Do you think God understands our feelings in those situations in which we feel incapable of forgiving? Does he allow us to remain unforgiving? Why or why not?

How might forgiveness actually set us free?

Video Notes

Debbie Morris: "The unforgiveness that I was holding on to, the hate, the anger, was destroying my life. I was continuing to let these men have control over me. I was continuing to let myself be victimized, over and over and over again, because I was hanging on to the hate and I was unwilling to forgive."

Tony Campolo: "I think we would all be gracious if we could look at each other and not see the enemy but see that each of us, in his or her own way, is somebody's little kid, sick and dying and far away from home. Grace."

Philip Yancey: "What incredible power—the linkage of the forgiver and the forgiven! In the truest acts of forgiveness, the wounded party eventually becomes a minister of love and a dispenser of God's grace."

Debbie Morris: "I know now that there's no such thing as unforgivable. And I've learned that mostly by taking little steps at a time."

Debbie Morris: "I think that many times people in my situation think that justice is what is going to heal them. . . . And I was disappointed time after time because justice was not fulfilling. What we get confused about is the healing effect of justice. Justice is not what heals us. . . . There's no such thing as justice here on earth for what that man did. . . . The only justice is going to be when God gives his final judgment."

Philip Yancey: "In the end [forgiveness] sets us free."

Bible Study

Joseph

Read Genesis 37:12–28, in which Joseph is sold into slavery.

1. How do you think Joseph felt toward his brothers after they sold him into slavery? On a scale of one to ten, how difficult do you think it was for him to forgive them?

Read Genesis 45:1–11, about Joseph's reunion with his brothers.

2. Joseph's story culminates with Joseph as governor of Egypt many years later. The land is experiencing famine, and his brothers have come to him seeking grain, unaware that he is their long-lost brother. Just prior to this passage, Joseph has experienced both great anger and great love for his brothers. Can you envision Joseph's struggle to forgive in light of the anger and love that each seemed overpowering? What do you think was going on inside his head?

3. Joseph was probably consumed by anger, and yet he felt moved to forgive and love his brothers anyway. What lesson can we learn from his example?

4. What do we learn about forgiveness and grace from these passages?

Bible Study

Peter

Read Mark 14:66–72, about Peter's denial.

1. How do you think Peter felt about denying Christ?

Read John 21:4–19, in which Jesus reinstates Peter.

Jesus asked Peter three times if he loved him. The first two times Jesus used the Greek word *agape* (self-sacrificial love), but the third time Jesus used the word translated *phileo* (brotherly love)—asking Peter, "Are you my friend?" Jesus doesn't settle for superficial answers. When Peter's response was, "Yes," Jesus said, "Feed my sheep." Jesus forgave Peter and restored him to the work Christ had for him to do.

2. What do we learn from Jesus about forgiveness? What do we learn from Peter?

3. What do we learn about forgiveness and grace from these passages?

Bible Study

Psalm 130

Read Psalm 130.

1. How does this psalm speak for the one needing forgiveness? How about for the one needing to forgive?

2. What part does waiting on God play? Should we forgive and then wait for God to supply the healing, or wait for healing and then forgive?

3. What does this psalm teach us about God's forgiveness?

Personal Reflection

In his book Philip writes,

The scandal of forgiveness confronts anyone who agrees to a moral cease-fire just because someone says, "I'm sorry." When I feel wronged, I can contrive a hundred reasons against forgiveness. *He needs to learn a lesson. I don't want to encourage irresponsible behavior. I'll let her stew for a while; it will do her good. She needs to learn that actions have consequences. I was the wronged party—it's not up to me to make the first move. How can I forgive if he's not even sorry?* I marshal my arguments until something happens to wear down my resistance. When I finally soften to the point of granting forgiveness, it seems a capitulation, a leap from hard logic to mushy sentiment.

1. What are my reasons for refusing to forgive another's wrongs against me?

2. Does God *ever* refuse to forgive me?

3. Why is it easier for me to accept God's forgiveness than to grant it to someone who has wronged me?

4. What will it take for me to be a more forgiving person?

Summary

In this session we:

- Considered how forgiveness is the only way in which to experience freedom from the deep wounds we carry.
- Explored some of the most difficult challenges to forgiving.

Suggested Reading

For more thoughts from Philip Yancey and more stories about grace, read:

What's So Amazing About Grace? chapters 8–9.

These chapters include an account of a discussion on forgiveness revolving around the case of mass murderer Jeffrey Dahmer, stories about unforgiveness in marriages, the story of a Ku Klux Klansman taken in and loved by a Jewish family, and the story of a German soldier who asked forgiveness of a Polish prisoner of the Nazis.

Looking for Grace Inside Myself

1. Has forgiveness ever felt, or does it feel now, nearly impossible with a particular person or situation in my life?

2. How can forgiving another in my life release me and free me in a way that can happen by no other means?

3. Is God's Spirit prompting me to forgive someone who has wronged me (in either a big or small way)?

4. Is there anything in my life I feel God can't forgive?

5. What steps do I need to take to let God have my brokenness?

6. Is God's Spirit prompting me to accept God's grace?

Pray for God's grace to fill your heart and mind as you contemplate his forgiveness for us which in turn affects our forgiveness of others.

SKIN-DEEP
THE POWER OF GRACE
TO PENETRATE RACISM

—⚬⚬⚬—

Questions to Consider

- In what ways do we see or experience racism in society today?

- What can we learn from the pain of those who have suffered from racism or any other kind of prejudice or mistreatment?

- How can our societal wounds be healed?

The Only Hope for Hatred

Where in our world are groups of people living in hatred of one another?

If there is any hope for healing these conflicts, what might that hope be?

Video Notes

Opening comment: "Some of the most intolerant people I know are Christians. I mean, I'm sorry to say that, but it's true."

Philip Yancey: "[Wiesel] began to see that although Christians may build walls between races and people, the real Jesus tears down the walls."

Patricia Raybon: "Race relations is about human relations. . . . Are we getting along is the wrong question. The question is, 'Are you my neighbor? Am I my brother's keeper? Am I my sister's keeper? No matter what color she is?' And if each of us would pose that question to ourselves, the larger question would be irrelevant."

Patricia Raybon: "When you forgive you rediscover the humanity of the other person. But even better, when you forgive you rediscover the humanity in yourself."

Patricia Raybon: "Forgiveness is hard . . . if you try to do it on your own, in your strength. . . . It goes against every moral and material law in the universe. So you're going to need some godly help to forgive. But you know what? That's okay."

Bible Study

Read Luke 10:25–37—the parable of the good Samaritan.

Samaritans were a mixed race produced when Jews from the northern kingdom intermarried with other peoples after Israel's exile. There was a deep hatred between the Jews and Samaritans.

1. What does this story teach us about our attitudes toward those who are different than we are and who we feel are inferior to ourselves?

2. Through this story, what did Jesus teach us about grace?

3. If Christians were to reach out to those around us, as did the good Samaritan, what would happen to our world?

A Collection of Attitudes

(taken from *The Life Application Bible.*)

To the expert in the law, the wounded man was a subject to discuss.

To the robbers, the wounded man was someone to use and exploit.

To the religious men, the wounded man was a problem to be avoided.

To the innkeeper, the wounded man was a customer to serve for a fee.

To the Samaritan, the wounded man was a human being worth being cared for and loved.

To Jesus, all of them and all of us were worth dying for.

Small Group Discussion

1. When addressing the issue of racism, which approach are you most likely to take?
   - Discussion
   - Exploitation
   - Avoidance
   - Financial gain
   - Love
   - Sacrificial giving

2. What does it take to get to the place of love and sacrificial giving? What role does grace play in our care for others?

3. Healing and change of any injustice come largely by peaceful opposition, forgiveness, and the continuing work of reconciliation. How is Jesus, the Son of the living God, the only hope for accomplishing these three things?

A Home for Bastards: A Story

(This is a shortened version of chapter 11 of *What's So Amazing About Grace?*)

In the 1960s, a Yale Divinity School graduate and Southerner named Will Campbell befriended a student named Jonathan Daniels. Campbell and Daniels were each involved in the civil rights crusade. Campbell's theology was undergoing some testing in those days. Much of the opposition to his civil rights work came from "good Christians." Campbell found allies more easily among agnostics, socialists, and a few devout Northerners.

"In ten words or less, what's the Christian message?" one agnostic had challenged him. The interlocutor was P. D. East, a renegade newspaper editor who viewed Christians as the enemy.

Campbell replied, "We're all bastards but God loves us anyway."

The definition stung P. D. East, who, unbeknown to Campbell, was indeed illegitimate and had been called "bastard" all his life. He put that definition to a ruthless test on the darkest day of Campbell's life, a day when an Alabama deputy sheriff named Thomas Coleman gunned down Campbell's twenty-six-year-old friend Jonathan Daniels.

That night Campbell spoke with P. D. East and got "the most enlightening theological lesson I ever had in my life." P. D. East pressed Campbell on whether his definition of faith could stand the test.

"Was Jonathan a bastard?" P. D. asked first. Campbell replied that though he was one of the most gentle guys he'd ever known, it's true that everyone is a sinner. In those terms, yes, he was a "bastard."

"All right. Is Thomas Coleman a bastard?" That question, Campbell found much easier to answer. You bet the murderer was a bastard.

Then P. D. pulled his chair close, placed his bony hand on Campbell's knee, and looked directly into his eyes. "Which one of these two bastards do you think God loves the most?" The question hit home, like an arrow to the heart.

Suddenly everything became clear. Everything. It was a revelation. . . . I began to whimper. But the crying was interspersed with laughter. . . . I was laughing at myself, at twenty years of a ministry which had become, without my realizing it, a ministry of liberal sophistication. . . .

I agreed that the notion that a man could go to a store . . . fire a shotgun blast at one of the customers, tearing his lungs and heart and bowels from his body . . . and that God would set him free is almost more than I could stand. But unless that is precisely the case then there is no Gospel, there is no Good News. Unless that is the truth we have only bad news, we are back with law alone.

What Will Campbell learned that night was a new insight into grace. The free offer of grace extends not just to the undeserving but to those who in fact deserve the *opposite*.

This message penetrated so deep inside Will Campbell that he resigned his position with the National Council of Churches and became what he wryly calls "an apostle to the rednecks." He bought a farm in Tennessee, and today is as likely to spend his time among Klansmen and racists as among racial minorities and white liberals. A lot of people, he decided, were volunteering to help minorities; he knew of no one ministering to the Thomas Colemans of the world.

Small Group Discussion

1. What impressed you most about this story?

2. What do you think of Will Campbell's summary of the Christian message: "We're all bastards but God loves us anyway"? Are you offended by the language? Have you ever felt anything like this—unworthy, illegitimate?

3. Read Romans 3:21–24. How would you paraphrase these verses in your own words?

4. What would you think of the idea of committing yourself to ministering to these kinds of people, as Campbell did to the Klansmen and racists?

59

Summary

In this session we:

- Identified the various ways in which racism rears it's ugly head in our world today.
- Listened to the stories of a Holocaust survivor and a victim of racism.
- Discussed the vital role Jesus plays in healing our deep societal wounds.

Suggested Reading

For more thoughts from Philip Yancey and more stories about grace, read:

What's So Amazing About Grace? chapters 10 – 11.

These chapters include the fascinating story of Philip Yancey's meeting in Russia, along with other Christians, with the KGB after the fall of the Soviet Union; an account of the racial climate in which Philip grew up; the humorous story of daring black South African women defending their village; and the story of one civil rights worker who came to terms with God's love for "bastards."

Looking for Grace Inside Myself

1. As a child, how did I feel about people who were of a different race or nationality? How have my views changed over time? Do I currently have any close friends from other races or nationalities?

2. In what ways have I contributed to the problem of racism?

3. How can I be a better listener and seek to understand those toward whom I feel anger or who are asking for my understanding?

4. What situation of injustice is God's Spirit prompting me to consider more carefully?

Pray that God would reveal to you how you can make an impact on racism—in a big or small way.

GRACE PUT TO THE TEST
GRACE IN THE FACE
OF DISAGREEMENT

Questions to Consider

- What impact should grace have on our relationships with those with whom we disagree strongly over important moral issues?

- How did Jesus treat morally impure people?

- What does the Bible teach us about our interactions with those with whom we disagree?

Growing a New Set of Eyes

What moral issues can you think of that are particularly divisive
among Christians today?

political
abortion
sexual discrimation
racial "

How do Christians usually treat other Christians with whom they
disagree on a moral issue?

"Tell me more about that."

What impact should grace have on our interactions?

Video Notes

Mel White: "When I say I'm an evangelical Christian, gay people turn away in disgust and evangelical Christians turn away in disgust. So there you are."

treating w/ grace

Philip Yancey: "It doesn't take grace to be kind toward someone you agree with. It can take a lot of grace to continue a relationship with someone you have trouble with."

Philip Yancey: "I learn a lot about how to treat people I disagree with by watching Jesus in action."

Philip Yancey: "When I come across a person I truly disagree with, I pray this prayer: 'Lord, help me not to see, "What a repulsive person. What an immoral person." Rather, help me to see, "What a *thirsty* person."'"

Mel White: "So for me, I don't ask Christians to accept me as a homosexual but to love me as a brother in Christ, and in the process of that kind of loving we'll both learn from each other."

Philip Yancey: "Ask for a new set of eyes—what I call grace-healed eyes. So that we see even people who offend us not just as immoral people but as thirsty people, like the Samaritan woman at the well."

Response Questions

1. What was your first reaction when you watched the clips of Mel White on the video?

2. Look at Philip's first quote on page 64. Do you agree or disagree with him?

3. What's the difference between "hating the sin" and "loving the sinner"? Why does the church so often fail at extending grace to those with whom we disagree?

4. Let's look at one other quote from today's video segment—Philip's first quote on page 65, about thirsty people. Can you imagine putting this prayer into practice in your own life?

5. What would happen in our own community if we were all to put into practice Philip's prayer?

Bible Study

1. Read Romans 3:21–24. According to these verses, what do all Christians have in common?

   What kind of differentiation is made regarding types or degrees of sin?

   What has been granted to us through Jesus Christ?

   Is there any stipulation on God's gift of redemption?

2. Read Colossians 4:5–6 and 1 Peter 4:7–11. Toward whom are we called to be gracious?

How do these commands reflect God's character?

3. Read John 17:20–23. What is Jesus' main concern in these verses?

How is the church doing today at exemplifying this highest desire of Jesus?

Small Group Discussion

1. We all have people with whom we disagree. What types of people are most challenging for you as you consider extending grace?
   - Fundamentalist Christians
   - Politically correct liberals *& extremists*
   - Wealthy conservatives
   - Feminists in the church
   - Pro-life or pro-choice advocates
   - "I need food" beggars along the road

2. Have you considered before your need to show grace to these people? How might you extend grace?

3. How should God's grace affect our interactions with people who hold different opinions, beliefs, or political positions?

4. Is there anything that is frustrating you about our discussions on grace? What are you finding to be encouraging or uplifting?

Summary

In this session we:

- Considered some of the greatest challenges in living out God's grace with those with whom we hold strong disagreement.
- Were introduced to some of the people with whom Jesus interacted, and considered how he expressed both his love and his disapproval.
- Discovered that God commands us in the New Testament to conduct ourselves toward others—both inside and outside the church—with love and compassion.

Suggested Reading

For more thoughts from Philip Yancey and more stories about grace, read:

What's So Amazing About Grace? chapters 12–13.

These chapters include the story of a children's sermon Philip preached; an explanation of God's Old Testament standard—no oddballs allowed—and the new rule of the New Testament; an account of Philip's friendship with Mel White; and the story of one church's outreach to the homosexual community.

Looking for Grace Inside Myself

1. What type of person am I most likely to label "repulsive" or "immoral" or "off-base spiritually"?

2. What is there about my thoughts and behaviors that would cause some Christians to feel a need for grace in their view toward me?

3. Is God's Spirit prompting me to begin seeing individuals in my life as thirsty people?

Pray that God would allow you to see those around you a thirsty persons.

GRACE ABUSE
CHEAPENING GRACE
AND ROBBING ITS POWER

⚬⚬⚬

Questions to Consider

- What is "grace abuse"?

- Does sin matter if we are eventually forgiven?

- How do grace and a commitment to holiness coexist?

An Uncomfortable Idea

What do you think the term "grace abuse" means?

How might a person abuse God's gift of grace?

Is there a limit to grace? What about when a person sins intentionally?

What incentive does a Christian have to be good, when he or she knows that the safety net of grace is always there?

Video Notes

Lewis Smedes: "Forgivers don't have to be fools. But they have to be willing to take a risk."

Philip Yancey: "[Jesus] saw sinners who admitted it ... and sinners who denied it. ... And the fact is, God can only work with people who admit their need."

Philip Yancey: "Grace is a gift. And the only way to receive a gift is to open your hands. If your hands are closed tight, like the older brother in the prodigal son story, so you think, *I'm doing just fine* . . . —the plain fact is that God's grace cannot help you."

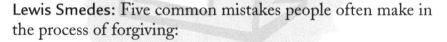

Lewis Smedes: Five common mistakes people often make in the process of forgiving:

1. Forgiving somebody is excusing them.

2. Forgiving is the same as tolerance.

3. People expect instant results.

4. You have to run to the person and tell them.

5. You've got to go back to the same relationship.

Small Group Discussion

1. Have you ever made a conscious decision to sin, with the thought of God's forgiveness in mind? What thoughts went through your head? What was the outcome?

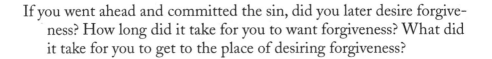

If you went ahead and committed the sin, did you later desire forgiveness? How long did it take for you to want forgiveness? What did it take for you to get to the place of desiring forgiveness?

2. Have you ever been called to show grace to someone in your life who was acting in obvious sin? How did you respond? What was their response to you?

3. Why is it so difficult for us to admit our faults, confess our sin, and repent?

Bible Study

1. Read Romans 6:1–2. Why would a person choose not to sin even though grace could be had afterward?

2. Read Romans 6:15–18. What does it mean to be a "slave to righteousness"?

3. Read Romans 6:22–23. What does God's grace produce in us?

4. Read Romans 7:5–7. What does it mean to "serve in the new way of the Spirit"?

5. In your experience, which is a more powerful motive for behavior— fear of punishment, or a desire to please someone you love? Does the Bible provide us with both motivations?

In his book Philip writes,

The best reason to be good is to want to be good. . . . If we truly grasped the wonder of God's love for us, the devious question that prompted Romans 6 and 7—What can I get away with?— would never even occur to us. We would spend our days trying to fathom, not exploit, God's grace.

6. Do you agree or disagree?

7. Read Colossians 3:12–17. How do these verses tie together grace and holiness?

Summary

In this session we:

- Considered grace abuse.
- Discussed why we should be good if we know God's grace will forgive.
- Examined several ways in which we can show grace while upholding holiness.

Suggested Reading

For more thoughts from Philip Yancey and more stories about grace, read:

What's So Amazing About Grace? chapter 14.

This chapter includes a story about a convict who murdered while in prison—so that he could die and be forgiven; a story about a friend considering divorce; a discussion of Paul's teaching in Romans; an account of a biologist's experiment with ants; and a story about German language lessons and romantic love.

Looking for Grace Inside Myself

1. Is there someone in my life that needs me to respond in grace to his or her conscious sinning? How is God's Spirit impressing me now to love this person?

2. Is there any conscious sin in my life that is killing a part of me and denying my love for God?

3. Where do I need to pry my fingers away from the rule book, open my hands, and admit to God my need for his grace?

4. How is God's Spirit prompting me to change my views on legalism? On holiness? On discipline?

Pray for God's wisdom as you try to discern his will for your attitudes, activities, and actions.

THE CHURCH BACKSLIDES
HOW LEGALISM
CORRUPTS GRACE

———— ⋘ ————

Questions to Consider

- What is legalism? *literal & too strict adhereance to rules rules*

- In what ways does legalism corrupt grace?
  lack of empathy become judgemental

- Why is legalism so destructive to the life of faith, the life of grace?

Going to Extremes

What is legalism?

If legalism is one extreme toward which the church moves at times,
what would be the other extreme?

What makes aspects of legalism appealing? — *easy*

can make on feel superior

Video Notes

Tony Campolo: "I think we have a bad rap. I think evangelicals are not as bad as their reputation. But their reputation is very bad."

Tony Campolo: "I think that the evangelical community has been so seduced into conservative politics that they have confused their political beliefs with the biblical message."

Tony Campolo: "We are all in a sense like the scribes and Pharisees and Saducees of old that take the Scriptures and they begin to spell out what that means in detail, and then we begin making very strong judgments about anybody that violates our understanding of the rules."

legalism = closed minds

Philip Yancey: "As I listened to those twelve steps [of Alcoholics Anonymous], they seemed to me to boil down to two big steps. One was radical honesty. . . . The second step was radical dependence."

Philip Yancey: "I know of only one good reason to go to church, and that's because I desperately need it."

Bible Study

Read Matthew 23:1–15, 27–28.

1. Why is Jesus so angry with the Pharisees?

2. The Pharisees were caught up in trying to impress each other, and in doing so they lost contact with the real enemy, as well as with the rest of the world. Who or what is the real enemy?

3. Read verse 15 again. What great caution must Christians today take when sharing the gospel and discipling, or teaching, new Christians?

Discussion Questions

In his book Philip writes,

Legalism is a subtle danger because no one thinks of himself as a legalist. My own rules seem necessary; other people's rules seem excessively strict.

1. Do you agree or disagree? What are some examples from your own life?

He also writes,

At first glance legalism seems hard, but actually freedom in Christ is the harder way. It is relatively easy not to murder, hard to reach out in love; easy to avoid a neighbor's bed, hard to keep a marriage alive; easy to pay taxes, hard to serve the poor. When living in freedom, I must remain open to the Spirit for guidance. I am more aware of what I have neglected than what I have achieved. I cannot hide behind a mask of behavior, like the hypocrites, nor can I hide behind comparisons with other Christians.

2. What do you find most difficult about freedom in Christ?

3. Concerning legalism, which of the following comes closest to describing you?

  • **A legalistic emphasis on externals:** I sometimes fall into the desire to impress others with my actions. I want people to feel I'm a deeply spiritual person.

  • **A legalistic extremism:** Better safe than sorry is how I sometimes feel. Like they say, "If you give an inch, they'll take a mile." I tend to want more rules so I and others don't stray from God.

  • **A legalistic emphasis on trivialities:** I care about the weighty matters, like justice and faithfulness, but feel overwhelmed by them. It's easier to control the smaller things, like dress and music. Sometimes I feel this is a manageable way of doing my part.

  • **An urge to rebel due to legalism:** I feel certain religious practices are important, but struggle with a spirit of rebellion against these practices.

  • **A legalistic sense of failure:** I struggle with feeling that I'm constantly failing God or have failed him in a big way in the past.

  • **Alienation from God due to legalism:** I struggle with relating to God due to the legalism in my past.

In another section of his book Philip writes,

Jesus proclaimed unmistakably that God's law is so perfect and absolute that no one can achieve righteousness. Yet God's grace is so great that we do not have to. By striving to prove how much they deserve God's love, legalists miss the whole point of the gospel, that it's a gift from God to people who don't deserve it. The solution to sin is not to impose an ever-stricter code of behavior. It is to know God.

4. What is the difference between knowing God and obeying his commandments?

Summary

In this session we:

- Defined legalism.
- Heard Philip Yancey's and Tony Campolo's perspectives on how legalism corrupts grace.
- Discussed the various ways in which legalism destroys our faith and our ability to show grace.

Suggested Reading

For more thoughts from Philip Yancey and more stories about grace, read:

What's So Amazing About Grace? chapters 15 – 16.

These chapters include an account of the legalism Philip Yancey experienced in Bible college; a pointed example of legalism as demonstrated by Tony Campolo; a confession by Henri Nouwen; and a true story of one man obsessed with morality and politics.

Looking for Grace Inside Myself

1. In what areas of my life is legalism actually easier than true freedom in Christ?

2. In what way am I influencing others in my life to buy into legalistic rules or concerns?

3. In what way is God's Spirit prompting me to lay down legalism and strive, through Jesus, to celebrate and live out freedom in Christ? In what way is God's Spirit prompting me to develop, not legalism, but godly discipline in my life?

Pray that God would show you where you need to have more of an attitude of grace.

DISPENSING GRACE
HOW CAN WE DO IT?

—⪻⪼—

Questions to Consider

- How should the Christian message be communicated in the political realm?

- In what ways are we "dispensers" of grace?

- What does God expect of Christians living in an evil society?

The Perfume of Grace

About what political issues of today are many Christians especially
concerned?

What are the different ways in which Christians demonstrate their
political views? Which are effective? Which are not?

Is it possible for Christians to effectively communicate disagreement
in the political realm in a graceful way?

Video Notes

Philip Yancey: "Now, completely apart from politics, I ask you, 'Which approach do you think communicates best? Those who yell and call names and wave placards, or those who approach with humility and grace?'"

Philip Yancey: "We dare not let our noisy involvement in power struggles drown our primary message: that of love."

Philip Yancey: "Grace can work like perfume. Spray a little in a crowded room, and it can change the complexion of the whole room."

Philip Yancey: "For people who feel obligated to clean up all the evil in the world, I have a word of encouragement: Relax. That's not our job. Not even Jesus attempted that."

Ann Spangler: "Grace looks at every individual with respect and with love and with the realization that they have the ability to know God, that there is something marvelous about the fact that they're a human being with the ability to make choices and think."

Philip Yancey: "The United States in the new millennium desperately needs the influence of Christians in our schools, our congressional halls, our justice buildings. I believe we will be most effective if we can carry a message into those places: the message of grace."

Bible Study

Read Matthew 13:24–30, 36–43 — the parable of the weeds.

1. What powerful words does Jesus use to describe the weeds and the one who sows them? What will be the outcome for the weeds?

2. How does Jesus feel about those whom the weeds represent? What does this say about how seriously he takes the wrongs that Christians and the Christian faith encounter?

3. What happens to the wheat? Does it get choked out or continue to grow amid the weeds?

4. How can this parable encourage us?

Small Group Discussion

1. If a government leader holds positions that you believe to be unbiblical, what do you feel is the biblical way to speak to and about that leader? To what extent are Christians responsible for determining whether a leader is truly a follower of Christ or not?

2. What do you feel is the biblical way to oppose policies you feel are unbiblical?

3. Is it possible for Christians to uphold moral values in a secular society while at the same time conveying a spirit of grace?

4. As you see our society veering away from God, with which of the following Bible characters do you tend to identify?

- **Elijah,** who hid in caves and made lightning raids on Ahab's pagan regime. I mostly stay in my Christian community but at times feel compelled to speak out, protest, or warn the secular community.

- **Obadiah,** who worked within the system, running Ahab's palace while sheltering God's true prophets on the side. I'm very much a part of secular society and feel this gives me knowledge, influence, and the opportunity to support fellow Christians.

- **Daniel**, who loyally served a heathen empire. I serve faithfully within the secular society yet try to let my Christian values permeate all I do. I hope never to compromise my beliefs to meet secular expectations.

- **Jonah,** who called down judgment on a heathen empire. I feel an urgency to tell our secular society that it is wrong and will be judged by God if it doesn't repent.

- **Esther,** who entered into a union with a heathen and through her godly spirit was able to save God's people. I have a lasting tie to an unbeliever and pray that God uses me in this person's life by revealing true faith through me.

- **Paul**, who appealed his case all the way to Caesar. I will go as far as necessary in the political realm to oppose unbiblical policies, acting respectfully yet passionately.

- If I'm honest with myself, at this time I'm really not trying to influence anyone for God.

5. How does a Christian go about choosing battles wisely?

Summary

In this session we:

- Considered how Christians can effectively communicate in the political realm.
- Were challenged by Philip Yancey to consider becoming a grace dispenser.
- Looked at what God expects of Christians living in an evil society.

Suggested Reading

For more thoughts from Philip Yancey and more stories about grace, read:

What's So Amazing About Grace? chapters 17–18.

These chapters include the story of Philip Yancey's *Christianity Today* article on Bill Clinton, and the responses he got; quotes by Andy Rooney, Randall Terry, and Ralph Reed; a discussion of C. S. Lewis's view on religion and politics; a discussion of Martin Luther King Jr.'s approach to confrontation; the example of Mother Teresa; and the story of a forum Philip attended in New Orleans during Mardi Gras season.

Looking for Grace Inside Myself

1. How have I thought about, spoken about, and/or acted toward political leaders whom I've disapproved of or disagreed with?

2. Do I sense God's Spirit prompting me to ask forgiveness for a wrong handling of a past situation? How can I respond now and in the future?

    Pray for God's Spirit to act through you in grace toward those who oppose God's ways.

COUNTERFORCE
GRACE SET LOOSE
IN THE WORLD

—∞∞∞—

Questions to Consider

- Is it realistic to hope that grace can be lived out in the most difficult of situations?

- How does God's kingdom operate?

- Does grace really make a difference?

This Swamp of a World vs.
the Kingdom of God

In our study of grace over the past few weeks, which situation has struck you as most challenging in the commitment to show grace?

Today we are going to talk about the kingdom of God. Can you think of any images Jesus used to illustrate the kingdom of God?

Video Notes

Gordon Wilson: "And I said, 'I bear them no ill will. I bear them no grudge. Dirty sort of talk is not going to bring Mary Wilson back to life. I shall pray for those guys tonight and every night that God will forgive them.' And I did. And I do."

Philip Yancey: "Grace is not some sweet, sentimental emotion that Christians feel at fleeting moments. It's a supernatural force of God set loose in a world ruled by its opposite, a world ruled by what I call ungrace."

Grace in:
The United Kingdom

The Middle East

South Africa

Philip Yancey: "Grace introduces something new: an awareness that the greatest things are all gifts. A newborn baby, the sunrise each day, rain falling on crops, romantic love, beauty—these are all gifts of God, common grace."

Philip Yancey: "The most powerful force any of us can ever show is the force that Jesus showed: sacrificial love."

Philip Yancey: "We are called to demonstrate sacrificial love to the world, to dispense God's grace. *But the world doesn't deserve it!* That's the point of grace. No one deserves it. It's free of charge, a gift of God, a counterforce against revenge and violence and evil."

Bible Study

Read Matthew 13:31–33—the parables of the mustard seed and the yeast.

1. How do you feel about letting God work in the world through his people in the same way a small bit of yeast works in bread, or a tiny seed in the ground grows into a tree?

2. What do these parables teach us about weakness and power? What do they say about hope in overwhelming situations?

Read Matthew 5:13–16, in which Jesus teaches about salt and light.

3. What does it mean to be salt and light in our world?

4. How do these verses relate to our discussions on grace?

Wrap-Up

1. As Philip stated in the video segment today, "[Grace] is ... a counterforce against revenge and violence and evil." How is this possible?

2. During our study of grace, what has impacted you most greatly?

3. As we have shared and studied together, how have you seen and experienced grace?

Summary

In this session we:

- Were reminded once again of the amazing power of grace in our world.

- Examined the way in which God's kingdom influences our world.

- Reflected on how God's grace has made an impact on our lives and our world.

Suggested Reading

For more thoughts from Philip Yancey and more stories about grace, read:

What's So Amazing About Grace? chapters 19–20.

These chapters include a story about the Mt. St. Helens' volcano; Philip Yancey's reflections on a trip to Russia after the fall of Communism; Philip's account of his participation in a panel that addressed the topic "Culture Wars"; and a story of dissidents in Eastern Europe.

Looking for Grace Inside Myself

1. As I think of the most difficult situation in my life, in which grace feels hardest to offer, I imagine God's grace, just the smallest bit of it, slipping into my being and affecting my response to this situation. What kind of effect could this bit of grace have?

2. What piece of my life needs God's grace as I leave this study and begin living in his grace?

3. What attitude is God's Spirit prompting me to submit to God?

Pray for God to continue to fill you with his grace that you might be a grace dispenser in all of your interactions: with family, friends, business associates, church members, neighbors, and government leaders.

ABOUT THE WRITERS

Brenda Quinn, formerly staff editor for Serendipity House and editorial coordinator for MOPS (Mothers of Preschoolers) International, Inc., is cowriter of study guides for *The Jesus I Never Knew* and *What's So Amazing About Grace?*

Sheryl Moon is a freelance writer. Her projects have ranged from designing a Christian education elective program for high school youth to writing guidebooks for video curriculum including the *Saving Your Marriage Before It Starts* curriculum by Drs. Les and Leslie Parrott, the *Capture the Joy* curriculum for Women of Faith, and the award-winning *The Jesus I Never Knew* curriculum by Philip Yancey. A graduate of Hope College and Western Michigan University, Sheryl lives in Grand Rapids, Michigan, with her husband and two children.

We want to hear from you. Please send your comments about this
book to us in care of zreview@zondervan.com. Thank you.

GRAND RAPIDS, MICHIGAN 49530 USA

ZONDERVAN.COM/
AUTHORTRACKER